MW00964418

The Sacrament of Reconciliation

Jesus Gives Us Peace

Written by
Claire Dumont
and Suzanne Lacoursière

Illustrated by
Gabrielle Grimard

Translated by Gisèle Larocque

Adapted by Irene C. Lapre

Pauline
BOOKS & MEDIA
Boston

Nihil Obstat: Rev. Christopher J. Coyne
Imprimatur: ✠ Most Rev. Seán O'Malley, O.F.M. Cap.
Archbishop of Boston
December 3, 2004

Library of Congress Cataloging-in-Publication Data

Dumont, C. (Claire), 1950-
   [Conduis mes pas vers la paix. English]
   Jesus gives us peace: the sacrament of reconciliation / written by Claire Dumont &
Suzanne Lacoursière ; illustrated by Gabrielle Grimard ; translated by Gisèle Larocque ;
adapted by Irene C. Lapre.— 1st English ed.
      p. cm.
   ISBN 0-8198-3984-1 (pbk.)
   1. Penance—Juvenile literature. 2. Confession—Catholic Church—Juvenile literature. I.
Lacoursière, Suzanne. II. Grimard, Gabrielle. III. Lapre, Irene C. IV. Title.
   BX2260.D8613 2005
   264'.02086—dc22

                              2004030494

Scripture texts in this work are taken from *The Holy Bible: Contemporary English Version,*
copyright © 1995, American Bible Society, 1865 Broadway, New York, NY 10023, and are
used by permission.

The Act of Contrition from the English translation of *Rite of Penance* © 1974, International
Committee on English in the Liturgy, Inc. (ICEL). All rights reserved.

English translation of The Apostles' Creed and Doxology by the International Consultation
on English Texts (ICET).

Originally published in French under the title *Conduis mes pas vers la paix* by Médiaspaul
3965, boul. Henri-Bourassa Est/Montreal, QC, H1H 1L1 (Canada)/www.mediaspaul.qc.ca/
Médiaspaul /48, rue du Four/75006 Paris (France)/media.arp@wanadoo.fr

First English edition, 2006

All rights reserved. No part of this book may be reproduced or transmitted in any form or
by any means, electronic or mechanical, including photocopying, recording, or by any
information storage and retrieval system without permission in writing from the publisher.

"P" and PAULINE are registered trademarks of the Daughters of St. Paul.

Copyright © 2003, Médiaspaul

Published by Pauline Books & Media, 50 Saint Paul's Avenue, Boston, MA 02130-3491.

Printed in Canada.

www.pauline.org

Pauline Books & Media is the publishing house of the Daughters of St. Paul, an international congregation of women religious serving the Church with the communications media.

1 2 3 4 5 6 7 8 9   12 11 10 09 08 07 06

Dear Children,

You are taking a special step in your life of faith by celebrating the *sacrament of Reconciliation* for the first time.

Because you are part of God's *big* family, your priest and your parish family invite you to experience this sign of God's great love, which is the sacrament of forgiveness. Congratulations! This is a time to thank God for all the wonderful things he does for you. It's also a time to tell God you are sorry for any wrong things you have done.

In getting ready to celebrate this sacrament, you have learned that it has many names. Two of the names we use the most are the *sacrament of Reconciliation* and the *sacrament of Penance.* It's also called the *sacrament of Peace,* or just *confession.* But no matter what we call it, this sacrament brings us God's forgiveness and peace.

It is not always easy to forgive. But God gives us the gift of forgiveness. When we have to forgive someone else for hurting us, it is God who forgives in us. We know that God loves us. God is always willing to forgive us. And he is always willing to help us forgive others.

Jesus has told us a very important secret. The secret is this: If we want to be happy, we must seek God's forgiveness when we sin. And we must forgive others as God forgives us. Jesus forgave many people when he was here on earth. Let's look at what Jesus did and try to act just like him.

We hope that you will let Jesus guide *your* steps toward peace with yourself, with others, and with God our Father.

Claire and Suzanne

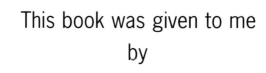

This book was given to me
by

on the occasion of the celebration of
the sacrament of Reconciliation,

which I received for the first time
on

at

.

Father

welcomed me in the name of Jesus.

(Sign your name.)

Autographs

I ask everyone who helped me to prepare to receive the sacrament of Reconciliation, and everyone who celebrated with me, to sign their name on this page as a remembrance of that special day.

**I have called you by name;
now you belong to me.**

(Isaiah 43:1)

I Am Important

My name is _____ .

I am _____ years old.

My mother's name is _____ .

My father's name is _____ .

I have _____ sisters.

I have _____ brothers.

My grandparents are _____ .

I like to _____ .

My favorite subject at school is _____ .

My favorite game is _____ .

My favorite book is _____ .

I Am Part of a Big Family

The first sign that I received to let me know
that God loves me was my Baptism.
My whole family celebrated this happy event.

It happened on

_____ .

at

_____ .

Photo
of my family

Photo
of my Baptism

My godmother is

_____ .

My godfather is

_____ .

I was baptized by Father

_____ .

Since the day of my baptism, I have been part of the great family of God's
children. This family, called the Church, is the community of Jesus Christ.

Before the priest baptized me with water, he welcomed me at the door
of the church and traced the Sign of the Cross on my forehead, inviting my
mother and father and godparents to do the same. This sign shows that
God loves me and that I belong to him. It confirms that I am a Christian.

I Belong to God!

God is the Father of all the people on earth. He wants to bring everyone into one big and beautiful family through his Son, Jesus.

God is Love. And Jesus, God's Son, came to earth to let us know this. Jesus even died on the cross because he loves us and wants us to live with God forever.

The cross is important for us. It reminds us of the love of Jesus and of his Father for each and every person. The cross is a sign of love.

You can thank God for the two special signs of love which he has given you so far: the sacrament of Baptism and the sacrament of Reconciliation.

After your prayer of praise, slowly make the Sign of the Cross. This gesture shows that you are happy to belong to God and that you want to remain Jesus' friend.

To me, you are very dear, and I love you.

(Isaiah 43:4)

Learning to Choose

God created us to love.

Jesus, who speaks in the name of God his Father, says to his friends: "Love God and love others as you love yourself."

Young or old, we are free to choose between what is right and what is wrong.

Each person has the power to do good deeds that *help* others or bad deeds that *hurt* others. We know that sometimes we choose what is wrong. Sometimes we choose *not* to answer God's call to love. When we purposely choose *not* to love, and we go against God or his Ten Commandments, we *sin*.

Any person who does not choose to do what is right is a *sinner*.

To Be Happy

When we love, we are happy!

When we love, we become more like God!

It is not easy to love as God loves. Many times we do just the opposite. We refuse to serve, to forgive, to share, and to help each other.

When you choose not to love, you do things and say things that hurt others.

This also hurts you. It may make you feel bad that you have hurt or offended someone else. It may make you feel guilty.

Has your friendship with someone ever been broken by unkind words or actions?

Feelings like fear, shame, or pride, or the feeling of no longer being loved can make it hard for you to forgive those who have hurt you.

*B*ut what about the times when you have hurt another person? The most important thing to think about then is not *what* you did, but *why* you did it. And the place to find out "why" is in the quiet of your heart.

You can make a mistake without meaning to do it. You can hurt someone by accident or on purpose.

Your heart will tell you the truth about the way you behave. And looking at the truth will help you to grow, to be happy, and to be peaceful.

Nothing Can Stop God from Loving You!

We have already told you how important you are and how much God loves you.

God loves you even when you know that something is wrong and you do it anyway.

We can be sure about this because Jesus, God's Son, has told us.

In the next few pages, you will read the stories of Peter and Mary Magdalene.

You will see the power of love that Jesus has in his heart.

Every mountain and hill
may disappear.
But I will always be kind
and merciful to you;
I won't break my agreement
to give your nation peace.

(Isaiah 54:10)

Two Good Friends

Jesus and Peter were good friends. Jesus had called Peter to follow him. They did many things together.

They went fishing. They visited the poor. They helped the sick. They prayed.

One day, Jesus' enemies decided to kill him. They didn't like what he was doing. They didn't like what he was saying. They thought he was causing trouble.

After the Last Supper, Jesus brought his closest friends to the Mount of Olives.

He asked Peter, James, and John to wait and pray with him.

Jesus was afraid of his enemies. He asked God his Father for help.

Jesus cried a lot. He felt alone.

He would have liked to talk with his three friends, but they were sleeping.

A troop of soldiers came to arrest Jesus. Peter wanted to defend Jesus with his sword. But Jesus would not let him. And Jesus went with the soldiers.

Peter was worried. He followed Jesus and the soldiers. While Peter was waiting in a courtyard to see what would happen to Jesus, some people recognized him. "Aren't you a friend of the man who was arrested?" a woman asked.

"I don't know what you're talk-ing about!" Peter answered.

Someone else said, "You were with Jesus."

Peter exclaimed, "I don't know that man!"

Then some other people in-sisted, "You are a follower of Jesus. We recognize you." And Peter denied Jesus again, saying, "I really don't know him!"

Not long after, some soldiers came by with Jesus.

Jesus looked sadly at Peter.

Then Peter understood the wrong that he had done to his friend Jesus. He went and hid himself and cried all night.

One beautiful morning, after his resurrection, Jesus went to meet his friends. They had spent the night fishing. But they had not caught anything. Jesus called out to them from the shore, "Throw your nets on the other side of the boat." Then John recognized Jesus. And Peter was so happy that he jumped into the water. The other apostles brought the boat ashore. Now the fishing net was full of fish!

Jesus had prepared a meal over a charcoal fire. He also cooked some of the fish that his friends had caught. He shared some bread and the fish with them.

After the meal, Jesus invited Peter to walk with him. He asked him twice, "Peter, do you love me?" Peter answered, "Yes, I love you."

But Peter became sad when Jesus asked him for a third time: "Do you love me?"

This time Peter answered, "You who know everything. You know that I love you." Then Jesus put Peter in charge of all his followers.

Peter was surprised that Jesus was giving him this important job—especially after he had lied three times and said that he didn't even know Jesus! Besides having forgiven Peter, Jesus still trusted him and wanted to be his friend. From then on, Peter did all he could to build the community that Jesus had started. We call this community the Church.

We Believe That...

Peter didn't want to deny that he knew Jesus. He only did it because he was afraid. When Jesus looked at him so sadly in the courtyard, Peter knew that he had done something really wrong. He had sinned. Peter felt sad, guilty, and ungrateful.

Peter only began to feel better after Jesus rose from the dead and came to talk to him. That's when Peter found out that Jesus' love for him was stronger than any of his sins. Jesus was still his friend! Peter's heart was filled with peace and joy.

What do you like the best about this story?

Prayer

Lord, teach me to look at others with kind eyes. Fill my heart with the love I need to forgive myself and those who hurt me.

Let Jesus Look at You

Mary Magdalene listened to the words of Jesus. She watched him from far away. She understood that Jesus was very special. Little by little, Mary began to want to change her life and become better. She wanted to meet Jesus, whose words did so much good.

One day a man named Simon invited Jesus to eat at his house. Jesus went in and sat at the table. There were many other guests there too.

When Mary Magdalene found out that Jesus was at Simon's house, she decided to go to see him. She walked into the house without having been invited. She was carrying a bottle of expensive perfume. The men who were there watched her angrily.

Mary started to cry. All she wanted was to see Jesus.

Simon and his friends felt like laughing and making fun of Mary. They knew that everyone in the town called her "the sinner." This was because Mary Magdalene had chosen to do some things that were wrong.

Jesus saw the unkind way that Simon and his guests were looking at Mary Magdalene. And he knew just what they were thinking. Jesus also saw everything that was in Mary's heart.

Mary Magdalene didn't care what anyone thought. Jesus was looking at her! She felt so happy. She went over and knelt in front of Jesus.

Mary let her tears fall on the feet of Jesus to wash them. She used her long hair to wipe them. Then she poured her expensive perfume on Jesus' feet.

Jesus welcomed Mary. He accepted her kind actions, which, according to Jewish custom, were done whenever guests arrived. Jesus looked at her and said, "Your sins are forgiven because of your great love. Go in peace."

By forgiving her, Jesus allowed Mary to feel good about herself again. She also felt good about being with others.

Mary Magdalene's heart was changed. She was full of peace and joy. From then on, she was able to make good choices. She chose things that made her grow and love and live in happiness.

We Believe That...

Mary Magdalene's actions show us how much she trusted Jesus. She felt welcomed and respected by him. She left Simon's house feeling very happy and peaceful.

Mary Magdalene believed that Jesus loves *everyone* without exception, in spite of their mistakes and their faults.

What do you like the best about this story?

Prayer

Lord Jesus, help me never to judge other people. I want to be like you and accept others and respect them in their differences. It's not always easy, but with your help, I will try.

May your Holy Spirit guide me on the road to peace and happiness.

**The Lord has worked
miracles
for his people.**

(Psalm 126:2)

Some Special Visits

Nicodemus, who was an expert in the religious laws, wanted to meet Jesus. He had questions to ask him. Jesus agreed to meet with Nicodemus.

They talked for a long time. Jesus told Nicodemus that God our Father does not judge or condemn people. God loves us all just as we are. And he wants us to live in the happiest way possible.

Another time, a tax collector named Zacchaeus climbed a tree so that he could see Jesus better. Jesus invited himself to Zacchaeus' house. Zacchaeus prepared a big dinner. He was proud to have Jesus come to his home. As he was listening to Jesus talk, Zacchaeus realized that he needed to change his way of life.

After that, he decided to share his riches with the poor and never to cheat anyone again.

Once some men brought their friend, who
had been paralyzed for a long time,
to see Jesus. They couldn't get into the
house because of the crowd, so they made
a hole in the roof. Then they lowered their
sick friend down on a stretcher.

Jesus was surprised by their great faith.
He said to the paralyzed man, "Your sins
are forgiven. Get up. Take your bed and go
home." The happy man went home
praising God.

Another time, Jesus told this story: A shepherd owned one hundred sheep. One ran
off and got lost. When he counted his
sheep that night, the shepherd realized
that one was missing.

After searching for many hours,
the shepherd heard the sheep crying.
He found it in a deep ditch. The
shepherd gently picked it up and car-
ried it on his shoulders. He spoke
softly to the sheep. He did not scold
it because it had run away.

The shepherd happily returned to his flock. He celebrated the finding of
his precious sheep with his friends.

By telling this story, Jesus wants to make us understand that God our
Father loves us no matter what we do!

"You must love each other, just as I have loved you."

(John 13:34)

Lauren and Bill

Lauren and Bill were just like their parents—they loved flowers! Lauren had even planted some beautiful flowers by the huge tree in their yard.

She went out every morning to water them.

One day, Bill asked Lauren to lend him her book on plants for his science project. Lauren said no because she needed it.

"Come on, Lauren," Bill moaned. "My project is due tomorrow!" But Lauren still wouldn't give him the book. "Give it to me right now, or I'll go step on your flowers!" Bill yelled. "No!" yelled back Lauren.

Bill ran out of the house—right toward the flowers! Lauren started crying as she watched him angrily trample her little garden.

At suppertime, Bill pouted. Lauren was still crying when she told their parents what had happened.

Mr. and Mrs. Holdridge listened. They understood that their children had acted out of anger. They asked Lauren and Bill to think of a peaceful solution to the problem.

Bill and Lauren went sadly to their rooms. Bill felt guilty.

Lauren was thinking of a way to get revenge when Bill knocked on her door. "Come in," she sighed. "Don't cry, Lauren," Bill said. "I shouldn't have done what I did. I'm sorry."

The next day, Bill told his parents that he wanted to make up for what he had done. His parents were happy. They even offered to buy him some new flowers.

After school, Bill ran home and planted the flowers for Lauren.

Lauren came home still feeling sad. She couldn't believe her eyes when she saw her beautiful new garden! She ran to find Bill. She gave him a hug. "Thank you!" she exclaimed. "I love you!"

Lauren and Bill felt happy and peaceful again. Their relationship had been restored. Their parents were happy too because Bill and Lauren had forgiven each other.

A Time to Forgive

*E*tty Hillesum, a young Jewish woman, died on November 30, 1943 at Auschwitz.

She spent the last months of her life in the concentration camp there.

She saw the people around her suffer very much.

But Etty tried to love everyone she met. She tried to love as God loves. She even went so far as to forgive the people who killed her.

*I*n 1981 a man tried to kill Pope John Paul II as he was blessing people who had come to see him.

After he got better, the Pope went to visit that man in prison. They talked for a long time. And Pope John Paul forgave the man.

Maria was 16 years old. One day, she saw men armed with guns shoot and kill her father, her mother, and her brothers—for no reason.

Maria suffered very, very much. She hated the men who had done this terrible thing.

It took many years before she was able to forgive them.

But with the help of God and the love of other people, Maria *did* forgive them. Then she felt peaceful again.

At recess, Nathan was attacked by three boys. They wanted his baseball cards. But Nathan wouldn't give them up.

The boys surrounded him, beat him, and stole all the cards.

Nathan felt afraid and helpless. He didn't know what to do. He decided to tell his mother everything—even though the bullies had told him not to. Nathan and his mother went to the school principal for help. The principal promised to meet with the troublemakers and their parents in order to put a stop to the bullying. He would also tell the boys that they had to get Nathan a new set of baseball cards.

Nathan accepted this solution. But he realized that it's not easy to forgive.

*D*raw a picture of a time when you have forgiven someone.

Draw a picture of a time when someone has forgiven you.

Prayer

God, our Father, help me never to take revenge, to hold a grudge, or to fight.

Let me talk about my problems with persons who can help me. Make me brave enough to speak up when someone is doing something wrong to someone else.

Make me an instrument of your peace.

Amen.

I, the LORD, will heal you and give you peace.

(Isaiah 57:19)

The Sacrament of Forgiveness and of Reconciliation

God wants peace for *all* the people on earth.

On Easter night, Jesus fulfilled his Father's wish by saying to his friends:

"Peace be with you!"

Then Jesus gave them the power to pass his peace on to others. Ever since that night, Jesus' Church has brought his peace to people through the sacrament of Reconciliation. This meeting with the priest allows us to celebrate God's unending love for us and to admit the ways we fail to love.

When we choose *not* to follow God's law of love, we sin. And when we sin, we lose the gift of peace. We can sin by *doing* things that hurt others or ourselves, or by *not doing* the good things that we should. Sin breaks our relationship with God and with other people.

We receive God's wonderful forgiveness and peace in the sacrament of Reconciliation. In fact, the sacrament is the *greatest* way in which we can experience God's forgiveness. We also receive something else that is very special: God's grace. Grace is the help that we need to live as God wants us to.

We celebrate the sacrament of Reconciliation in **six** steps:

1. We *think* of our sins.
2. We are *sorry* for them.

3. We *confess* (tell) our sins to the priest.

4. We *promise* Jesus that we will try not to sin again (the Act of Contrition).

5. The priest gives us God's forgiveness through a prayer called "absolution."

6. We do or pray the *penance* the priest gives us.

*T*he priest listens to us. He gives us good advice. Then he tells us, in the name of Jesus: "You are forgiven. Go in peace!"

This means that it's our turn to bring forgiveness and peace to everyone we live with.

*W*e can also receive forgiveness through prayer, through acts of kindness and love, or by apologizing to the person whom we have offended. Our desire to make up for the wrong things we do comes from the Holy Spirit. In one of the letters we find in the Bible, St. Peter writes: "Above all, always have love for one another because love covers a great number of sins."

When you go to the sacrament of Reconciliation, it's good to talk to the priest about anything that is bothering you. Besides giving you God's forgiveness, he can help you find solutions to your problems. He can also give you good advice that will help you to become more like Jesus.

You don't have to worry; the priest will keep your secrets!

We know how much God loves us. We also know how hard it can be for each of us to love other people and to do what is right sometimes. It is good to pray for God's help and forgiveness as part of his big family.

That is why our parish community invites us to celebrate the sacrament of Reconciliation *together* at special times of the year, like Christmas and Easter.

Prayer

God, Father of Jesus and our Father,
You have given us every good thing we have, especially our life, our family, and our wonderful world.
Help us to take care of all your gifts and to share them with love. Help us to come and ask your forgiveness when we do not love and share as we should. Amen.

Change My Heart

It's not always easy to keep our promises to do better. This is why we need to ask the Holy Spirit to help us. He will show us how to choose things that will make us and other people happy.

Saint Francis of Assisi has given us a beautiful prayer that we can say:

Lord, make me an instrument of your peace!

Where there is hatred, let me sow love.

Where there is injury, let me sow pardon.

Where there is disagreement, let me sow unity.

Where there is doubt, let me sow faith.

Where there is error, let me sow truth.

Where there is despair, let me sow hope.

Where there is sadness, let me sow joy.

Where there is darkness, let me sow light....

Lord, make me an instrument of your peace!

Mary and Joseph

In the Gospels we read about Mary, the mother of Jesus, and Joseph, his foster father. We can learn many good things from the lives of Mary and Joseph. These good things are called *virtues*. When we practice virtues, they help us to grow as persons. They also help us to get along well with others.

Here are some virtues we can learn from the lives of Mary and Joseph:

Trust	Being careful in our work
Kindness	Friendliness
Respect	Truthfulness
Helpfulness	Forgiveness
Peacefulness	

Which one of these virtues would you like to practice more?

_____

Athletes need to practice their sport in order to become really good at it. You also need to practice the virtue you want to develop in your life.

Prayer

Mary and Joseph,
please help me to practice
the virtue of

_____ .

Please give me the courage
to live it every day,
even if my friends sometimes
make fun of me
for doing what is right.

Help me to love myself
and others so that
I may always act
like your Son, Jesus.

Amen.

A Plan for Happiness

One day, when crowds of people had come to see him, Jesus climbed a mountain. He sat down and began to speak to the people. He taught them how to be happy. He teaches us too. Here is what Jesus said about being happy:

God blesses those people who depend only on him.
They belong to the kingdom of heaven!
    ...because they have learned that we can trust God our Father.

God blesses those people who grieve.
They will find comfort!
    ...because they have learned that gentleness is more powerful than violence.

God blesses those people who are humble.
The earth will belong to them!
    ...because they know that God is our comfort and that he will send us kind persons to help us.

God blesses those people who want to obey him more than to eat or drink.
They will be given what they want!

...because they know that it is good to share and to respect the rights of others.

God blesses those people who are merciful.
They will be treated with mercy!
...because they try to lessen the suffering of others.

God blesses those people whose hearts are pure.
They will see him!
...because by being good and kind they have learned to see God in other people.

God blesses those people who make peace.
They will be called his children!
...because by being at peace with themselves and with other people they fulfill the wish of Jesus: "Peace be with you."

God blesses those people who are treated badly for doing right.
They belong to the kingdom of heaven.
...because they walk humbly under the loving gaze of God our Father.

(See Matthew 5:3–11)

Words That Do Good

God tells me:
You are important to me. I love you as you are.
There is no one else like you in the whole universe.
You are my beloved son. You are my beloved daughter.

What else does God tell you?

My father or my mother tells me:
I love you.
You are very special to me.
I am proud of you.

What else do they tell you?

My friends tell me:
I really like playing with you.
You are my best friend.
I'm happy when you can help me with my homework.

What else do they tell you?

Let's Give Thanks!

We invite you to say this prayer of thanks with your family to celebrate any happy event:

Let's praise the Lord for all his wonders!

For the light that brightens the day,	*we praise you, Lord!*
For the rain that nourishes the soil,	*we praise you, Lord!*
For the bread that makes us strong,	*we praise you, Lord!*
For the trees that shelter the birds,	*we praise you, Lord!*
For the moon that lights the night,	*we praise you, Lord!*
For the greatness of the ocean,	*we praise you, Lord!*
For all living things,	*we praise you, Lord!*

Let's praise the Lord for all his wonders!

For the happy times we share,	*we praise you, Lord!*
For comfort in times of sadness,	*we praise you, Lord!*
For the friends who bring us joy,	*we praise you, Lord!*
For the peace that is your gift,	*we praise you, Lord!*
For the freedom to make choices,	*we praise you, Lord!*
For all acts of forgiveness given and received,	*we praise you, Lord!*
For the love found in the hearts of all people,	*we praise you, Lord!*

Let's praise the Lord for all his wonders!

For the Church, the large family of
God's children,   *we praise you, Lord!*

For all persons who do good to others,   *we praise you, Lord!*

For those who do not love us,   *we praise you, Lord!*

For all the people on earth,   *we praise you, Lord!*

Continue the prayer of praise with your own words.

For _____

For _____

For _____

For _____

Let's praise the Lord for all his wonders!

In Conclusion...

Dear young friends,

It will make us very happy if this book helps your faith and love of God grow.

We encourage you to share with your parents, with your grandparents, and with your whole family what you have learned and remember from the stories you have read. You could ask them to pray with you, too.

We'd also like to share a secret with you: the way to be *really* happy is to give life to others. How do we do this? By doing good deeds. Here are a few examples:

- choose kindness instead of violence;
- avoid saying words that hurt;
- help your parents, your brothers and sisters, and your friends;
- take care of yourself by eating the right foods, sleeping well, and exercising;
- protect your environment and work to keep it beautiful.

These actions make life grow in you and help you to spread life, peace, and happiness everywhere.

If you behave in this way, you are following the advice that God gives us in the Bible: "Choose life." Jesus told his friends something similar: "I came so that my sheep may have life in abundance." With Jesus, let's always try to choose life. Life has been given to us as a gift so that we can give it to others as a gift.

We are close to you through our faith in God, our love for Jesus, and through prayer. We hope that you will always choose life, so that peace may spread in your heart, in your family, in your class, in your country, and in the world! *Be happy!*

Claire and Suzanne

Prayers

The Sign of the Cross

In the name of the Father, and of the Son, and of the Holy Spirit. Amen.

Our Father

Our Father, who art in heaven, hallowed be thy name. Thy kingdom come. Thy will be done on earth as it is in heaven. Give us this day our daily bread, and forgive us our trespasses, as we forgive those who trespass against us. And lead us not into temptation; but deliver us from evil. Amen.

Hail Mary

Hail Mary, full of grace, the Lord is with you. Blessed are you among women and blessed is the fruit of your womb, Jesus. Holy Mary, Mother of God, pray for us sinners, now and at the hour of our death. Amen.

Glory

Glory to the Father, and to the Son, and to the Holy Spirit: as it was in the beginning, is now, and will be for ever. Amen.

The Apostles' Creed

I believe in God, the Father almighty,
    creator of heaven and earth.
I believe in Jesus Christ, his only Son,
    our Lord.
        He was conceived by the power of
        the Holy Spirit
        and born of the Virgin Mary.
He suffered under Pontius Pilate,
        was crucified, died and was
        buried.
He descended to the dead.
On the third day he rose again.
He ascended into heaven,
        and is seated at the right hand
        of the Father.
He will come again to judge the
        living and the dead.
I believe in the Holy Spirit,
    the holy catholic Church,
    the communion of saints,
    the forgiveness of sins,
    the resurrection of the body,
    and the life everlasting. Amen.

Act of Contrition

My God,
I am sorry for my sins with all my
        heart.
In choosing to do wrong
and failing to do good,
I have sinned against you
whom I should love above all things.
I firmly intend, with your help,
to do penance,
to sin no more,
and to avoid whatever leads me to sin.

Our Savior Jesus Christ
suffered and died for us.
In his name, my God, have mercy.